Original title:
Whispers of the Tidepool

Copyright © 2025 Creative Arts Management OÜ
All rights reserved.

Author: Victor Mercer
ISBN HARDBACK: 978-1-80587-367-9
ISBN PAPERBACK: 978-1-80587-837-7

Chronicles of the Fisherman's Heart

A fish sneezed, oh what a mess,
Splashes flying, none to impress.
Casting nets with laughter loud,
Hooked a boot, was quite a crowd.

The crabs all danced, their little feet,
Doing the cha-cha on the street.
With every cast, the tales grow tall,
Even the seagulls laugh and squall.

The Elegy of the Swaying Seaweed

Seaweed wiggles to a tune,
Dancing 'neath the bright, round moon.
An octopus, with flair so grand,
Wears a hat made of pure sand.

The jellyfish float, a silly sight,
Glow-in-the-dark on a starry night.
Bubbles pop, then giggles spread,
As krill play tag above their bed.

Threads of Life Underwater

Anemones tickle fish galore,
While clownfish shout, "We want more!"
Bubble-blowing, they puff with glee,
Chasing shadows, wild and free.

Sea stars twirl on the sandy floor,
Trying ballet, oh what a score!
With each splash and swirl, they promote,
Underwater antics, quite remote.

The Silence of Sapphire Depths

A whale whispered to a clam,
"Let's start a shellfish jam!"
Turtle joined with a goofy grin,
"Can I get in on the spin?"

The sea cucumbers brought snacks too,
"Tofu surprise, I made for you!"
Bubbles echo in laughter's spread,
As they groove in their ocean bed.

Whispering Algae and Cousin Coral

In a pool where the green stuff grows,
Cousin Coral hums, striking a pose.
'Is that a wave or just your hair?'
Algae giggles, 'I'm beyond compare!'

Bubbles dance, a silly jig,
Crabs laugh hard, they're quite the gig.
'Hey, Algae, got jokes to share?'
'Only if you promise not to stare!'

Sea cucumbers lend their ear,
'We love your humor, bring us cheer!'
Coral jests, 'Don't be crass,
Or I'll throw you out on your... grass!'

Stories Carried by Seafoam

A sea snail tells tales with a grin,
'Last week, I got stuck in a tin!'
The seafoam whispers, 'What a sight!'
And laughs as the gulls take flight.

Starfish roll on the sandy ground,
'Bet you can't jump like us around!'
The wave crashes, 'In this I excel!'
While fish snicker, 'Do tell, do tell!'

With shells as microphones, they sing,
Comedy's the funny, salty fling.
'Catch my drift? I'm on a roll!'
Crabs reply, 'Focus on your stroll!'

Petals of an Ocean Bloom

Anemones blow kisses to the breeze,
While sea urchins giggle with tease.
'Look at my petals, aren't they neat?'
'They're lovely,' says the clam, 'not a treat!'

The clownfish join in with a dance,
'We'll twirl and twist, come take a chance!'
A seaweed garland bobs along,
'This underwater party can't go wrong!'

But jellyfish float with graceful flair,
'I'm just here to shock and scare!'
The others laugh, 'Not today, my friend,
Your surprises are where fun ends!'

Beneath the Crustacean Canopy

Under the rocks where shadows play,
Crabs create games, ravishing and gay.
'Who can scuttle the fastest, hey?'
Clams chime in, 'And let's eat, hooray!'

Among the seaweed, laughter erupts,
A hermit crab shouts, 'That's what's up!'
While shrimp share tales of mischief and spree,
'Let's have an epic crustacean jubilee!'

The tide takes a break as they regale,
Silly stories swirling like a whale.
'If I wore your shell, would I get a laugh?'
'You'd probably just crack it in half!'

Waters of Ancients and Their Echoes

In a pool where sea critters feast,
A crab in a bow tie looks like a beast.
With a wink and a wave, he's quite the charmer,
Declares himself king, all others are armor.

A fish in a top hat dances around,
Shoes too big, he trips and is bound.
A clam claps its shell, what a sight to see,
"May I join the ball?" cries the shrimp with a plea.

Seaweed wiggles, the starfish plays nice,
While octopuses juggle with finesse and spice.
Laughter bubbles up, it's a jolly parade,
As the tidepool erupts in a hilarious charade.

Horizons of the Untamed Sea

On the shore, a seal steals a shoe,
Riding the waves, he thinks it's brand new.
With a flip of a flipper, he glides with glee,
"Just call me the king of the wavy spree!"

A gull reports news with a honk and a lob,
"I lost my lunch, what a terrible job!"
While a sea turtle dreams of land with a tan,
"I'll crawl there tomorrow, I can, I can!"

Barnacles gossip on a bright rock stage,
"Did you hear the shrimp is now turning a page?"
Their tales spun in bubbles, each laughter a twist,
A sticky situation, how could they resist?

Vestiges of a Forgotten Lagoon

The ancient fish tell stories from long ago,
Of jellyfish parties, and tidal flow.
"Oh, remember the jelly?" a shrimp starts to laugh,
"Dipped in salsa, what a culinary craft!"

A sponge with a grin claims to be a chef,
"Should I sauté or just serve 'em fresh?"
The sea urchins giggle, quite hard to withstand,
"Just don't let him use that seaweed band!"

With bubbles and gurgles, they toast with a cheer,
To the fish that survived all these foolish years.
In the lagoon's embrace, they splash and they twirl,
Living legends together, in a riotous whirl.

Cerulean Stories Told in Whirls

In a cerulean whirlpool, all dressed in blue,
A clownfish dressed up and is acting brand new.
With juggling sea stars who throw glittery stones,
"It's not a fish tale, just borrowing bones!"

A dolphin flips high, yells, "Watch my new trick!"
"Just don't belly flop; it'll hurt quite a bit!"
With laughter erupting, the bubbles do rise,
Echoes of joy, beneath sparkling skies.

The tide brings a dance, of laughter and fun,
As the creatures unite, with a wink and a run.
In the depths they find treasures, not silver nor gold,
Just stories and giggles, worth more than told.

Melodies from the Undersea Garden

In the garden beneath the waves,
Shells speak secrets, oh how they rave.
The starfish sings on a clamshell stage,
While sea cucumbers dance, wild and sage.

A crab in a tux, feeling so spry,
Trips on a seaweed tie, oh my!
The octopus juggles, all eight in a row,
With a giggle and squirt, putting on a show.

Fish in bowties swim by in a flash,
Sardines giggle, "Oh, what a splash!"
The seahorse whispers, "Let's have a ball!"
With bubbles and laughter, they invite us all.

In this frolicsome scene, fun never fades,
With jellyfish glow and bright promenade.
Every wave carries a chuckle or cheer,
Underwater antics, let's all come near!

Legends Linger in the Aquamarine

Old turtles tell tales of days long past,
In the depths where shadows are cast.
With a puff of their gills, they start to narrate,
How eels set up pranks, oh how they create!

"Beware of the puffer," says one with a wink,
"He's quite the character, more than you think!"
The clownfish snickers, recounting a jest,
While sea urchins point, they love to invest.

A mermaid giggles, "I've lost my shoe!"
"Check under a rock, it's hiding from you!"
The shells all crack up; everyone's in on the fun,
As barnacles chuckle, "You're not the only one!"

In this world of legends, laughter unfolds,
As krill tell their stories, so silly and bold.
The mysteries come alive in a fit of delight,
As we dance with the waves through the starry night.

Crafting Memories on the Coastline

Building castles from sand, what a delight,
With buckets and shovels, we're ready for flight.
The seagulls debate if they should come steal,
Our snacks from the towel – it's their best meal!

With shells as our treasures, we'll fill up the pail,
Swap stories of crabs that once rode a whale.
A starfish declares, "Saltwater's my drink!"
While we laugh so hard, we can hardly think.

The tide tickles toes as waves roll around,
"Surf's up!" shouts the dolphin, with flips and a bound.
Sand in our sandwiches, laughter and cheer,
A picnic of joy with good friends near.

As sunsets paint skies in magical hues,
We sculpt silly memories, each one like a muse.
With splashes and giggles, we bid the day bye,
In the glow of the stars, our laughter will fly!

Reflections of the Tide

The seaweed sways, a wobbly dance,
Crabs in a conference, plotting their prance.
Starfish play cards, they're quite the guys,
Cheating with tentacles, oh what a surprise!

Jellyfish giggle, float like a kite,
While clams time their claps, so perfectly tight.
Anemones jive, their colors aglow,
Making a splash in this watery show!

Seashells gossip about sunken ships,
With tales of treasure and daring trips.
The tide stirs up laughter in every wave,
A spectacle grand, the ocean misbehaves!

In this salty world, joy knows no bounds,
As fish throw a party, with bubbly sounds.
The sea, a stage for a show full of glee,
Where everyone knows it's better to be free!

Beneath the Surface of Stillness

A bubble of laughter hides in the sea,
Where turtles discuss who's the best at spree.
They're zippy and quick, with shells on their backs,
Taking bets on who will trip the most cracks!

Octopus artists paint with great flair,
Creating a mural, oh what a rare!
They giggle with ink, as colors they blend,
Drawing real mermaids, who always pretend!

Fish with sunglasses swim by nonchalant,
Doing the worm, in a synchronized chant.
They know how to groove, not a care in sight,
In their underwater disco, it's all sheer delight!

The lobsters are at it, showing off claws,
Strutting like models, they break all the laws.
With each little wave, more tales will unfold,
A splash of pure laughter, brave and bold!

Epiphanies of the Aquatic World

A dolphin named Dave took a leap and then —
He landed right next to a group of zen men.
Meditating fish giggle and float,
While sea cucumbers try to take note!

Crabs crack jokes with a pinch of sass,
About funny blunders they see as they pass.
Seahorses prance in a leisurely glide,
Making fun of the eel who just can't hide!

Mussels throw parties, with bubbles and cheer,
Inviting the clams for a dance near the pier.
Their party hats made from the best ocean finds,
Celebrating the tides with their bubbly backsides!

And all of the creatures, both big and small,
Share laughter and joy, yes, they all fall.
A celebration of life, beneath foamy sprawl,
In the colorful depths where humor stands tall!

The Heartbeat of the Sea

In a swirl of shells, the sea plays its tune,
With each silly wave like a playful balloon.
The seagulls squawk, and the otters are slick,
Chasing each other, and pulling a trick!

A fish with a mustache wears quite the style,
He twirls through the water, swimming a mile.
All the shrimp cheer him, their hero so brave,
While the barnacles laugh, hiding under the wave!

A crab with a hat gives a speech with great flair,
"I declare today, it's 'Dress Fancy' down here!"
The torpedoes swarm, in a rainbow parade,
Showing their best, oh how they're displayed!

As the sea brushes rocks, it hums soft and sweet,
Creating a rhythm that dances on feet.
In the miracle tide — a world so absurd,
Where laughter and joy can truly be heard!

Harmonies of Liquid Light

Bubbles giggle, fish do dance,
Seaweed sways, it's quite a prance.
Hermit crabs in homes they roam,
Crawling in their borrowed foam.

Starfish play hide and seek, oh dear,
While clams clam up, they shed a tear.
Anemones wave, they look so spry,
Dancing in the tide, oh my, oh my!

Jellyfish float like balloons of glee,
Who invited them to this jubilee?
Porpoises laugh, with flips in the air,
And everyone's welcome to join the fair!

So come take a peek at this ocean floor,
Where the party keeps rolling, and we ask for more.
With each splash and giggle, the fun won't fade,
In this watery world, new friendships are made.

Unseen Voices of the Estuary

Crabs chit-chat in sandy bars,
While seagulls gossip about the stars.
Oysters giggle, all tucked inside,
With clams quipping, 'We just texted tide!'

Frogs croak tunes under moonlit skies,
As fish murmur their sweet goodbyes.
Mudskippers flaunt their funky moves,
Boogie in the mud, they've all got grooves!

Snails wear hats made of shells and grass,
While otters tumble, just having a blast.
The currents carry tunes both near and far,
As dolphins sing a raucous guitar!

In these waters, no one is shy,
The loudest voices swim and fly.
Join the revelry in this liquid spree,
With laughter and music, feel so carefree.

Soft Footfalls on Sea Glass Shores

Beachcombers shuffle, with eyes on the ground,
Searching for treasures, a rare find is found.
Tiny bits of glass that glitter and shine,
Transform all the debris into gems so divine.

Seagulls squawk, "What's that glint?"
While children giggle, their footprints print.
Each tiny castle through laughter builds,
As waves rush in, all excitement spills.

Waves crash wild with a splashy swoosh,
Kids slip and slide; "I just did a whoosh!"
"Can we take home this wet, sandy beach?"
"Let's make a mud pie!" "Don't forget to teach!"

The sand tickles toes; the sun gives a wink,
As the playful tide bubbles, bubbles it pink.
Every corner shines with stories to score,
With memories forged on this vibrant shore.

Fleeting Moments of Sea Breeze

With every puff of salty air,
The crabs exchange a secret stare.
The wind whispers tales of old sea fights,
As surfboards ride the playful heights.

Seashells gossip on the sandy dunes,
While dolphins dance and sing their tunes.
Squids on scooters make quite a scene,
Wearing shades and eating ice cream.

Kites soaring high, like fish in flight,
As the seagulls dive for a tasty bite.
Breezes chuckle, swirling through grass,
While the sun casts shadows that quickly pass.

Oh, what a world where laughter flows,
In swirling tides and ocean shows.
Each breath of breeze is a moment caught,
A joyous dance in this seaside plot.

Voices Beneath the Surf

Beneath the waves, the seaweed sings,
A crab in slippers and a starfish king.
They gossip 'bout fish, make silly bets,
Who's the fastest swimmer? Place your pets!

The clams clap shells in a goofy dance,
Poking fun at the octopus's pants.
The sea cucumber chuckles at a shell,
Telling tales of how it once fell.

The jellyfish jokes with a fluid grin,
"Catch me if you can!" as he floats in.
The seahorse struts in a bright bow tie,
Winking at the flounder swimming by.

With laughter echoing from sandy shores,
The ocean's party never bores.
Splashing and tumbling, it carries on,
Beneath the sun, from dusk to dawn.

Charm of the Tidal Pools

In pools of water, the gobies play,
Building castles from sand every day.
A snail speeds in, yelling, "What's the rush?"
While the sea urchins giggle in a hush.

A crab in a crown thinks he's quite grand,
While a limpet complains, "I need more land!"
Starfish pretend they're painting the rocks,
As barnacles dance in their little socks.

Oysters compete for the shiniest shell,
Trading secrets they'll never tell.
As tides shift, laughter fills the air,
Oh, the fun found in this salty lair!

Creatures chat as the sunlight wanes,
In the charm of pools, life never wanes.
With laughter and smiles from all around,
Joy in the tides is abundantly found.

Enigmas of the Shifting Sands

The sands, they shift like a sneaky cat,
Hiding seashells and the odd beach hat.
A crab plays hide-and-seek with the tide,
While seagulls squawk, "Where's the fish?" with pride.

Dunes wave hello, then hide in a wink,
Telling the otters, "Give this a think!"
Beneath the grains, secrets are spread,
While the little sand dollars lie in bed.

A tumbleweed rolled with a silly cheer,
Said, "What's this mess? Let's all draw near!"
As the tide laughs at the sandy pranks,
The ocean chuckles, giving thanks.

With every wave that kisses the shore,
Life's little riddles bring us back for more.
In shifting sands, we discover anew,
The funny side of the ocean's view.

The Collage of Coastal Life

A collage unfolds on the sandy shore,
Where jelly beans bounce, and surfboards soar.
Seagulls take selfies with a good backdrop,
As happy fish twirl in a splashy flop.

Sand crabs are sketching, it's quite the sight,
Drawing flip-flops on a warm summer night.
The otters are posing, striking a pose,
While the clams roll their eyes, an art world knows.

The anemones wave with a pastel twist,
"Join our art class!" they insist with a fist.
Painting all day under the bright sun,
Creating a scene that never is done.

In this vibrant art, life takes a bow,
Each creature's a brush, making waves somehow.
With laughter around, we all come alive,
In the collage of life, we happily thrive.

Harmony in the Coastal Breeze

Seagulls squawk with cheerful glee,
As crabs do tap dance near the sea.
Starfish flex in Sunday best,
While clam shells laugh at their own jest.

The dolphins dive with playful grace,
Chasing fish in a frantic race.
A seaweed wiggle, quite absurd,
Makes the grouchy fish disturbed.

Octopuses pose for selfies too,
With eight arms waving 'Look at you!'
Sand dollars giggle as they hide,
While little kids run, laughing wide.

The tide rolls in with a joyful hum,
Mixing foam and sand like bubblegum.
What a silly scene, it seems they know,
The ocean's laughter as they put on a show.

Lingering Notes of Aquatic Hymns

A fish in a tux, what a funny sight,
Trying to dance by the moonlight.
Sea turtles skate on shimmering tides,
Bouncing off waves as the laughter glides.

A crab sings loudly, off-key and proud,
While clams keep beat, reinforced by the crowd.
Barnacles tap to the rhythm of foam,
Creating a tune that feels just like home.

Little shrimps twirl like ballerinas,
Under bright lights, their own arenas.
The ocean's choir, a cacophony,
Of fishy jokes and goofy harmony.

They whistle tunes about lost boots,
And argue about the best sea fruits.
In this wacky world, they find their bliss,
Amidst the bubbles and a cheeky kiss.

Shores of Forgotten Dreams

Upon the beach, old flip-flops sigh,
As crabs march on, with heads held high.
Sandy castles, all crumbly and weak,
Stand proud like warriors, proud to speak.

A beach ball floats, full of despair,
As jellyfish dance without a care.
Driftwood whispers tales of past,
Of surfboards and surfers, wild and fast.

Seashells giggle, all in a row,
As sea cucumbers put on a show.
Octopuses juggle, making a mess,
While tides roll in to clean the excess.

A dolphin croons a long-lost song,
While starfish marvel, 'What could go wrong?'
In this sandy realm, absurd and bright,
Dreams play the day away, just right.

The Solitude of the Sand

The grains of sand have thoughts of gold,
In a soap opera that's never told.
Footprints chase one another's tracks,
While the waves giggle and splash their backs.

A sand crab fiddles with its own shell,
Feeling quite dandy, it does quite well.
The starfish argue over the best spot,
While seashells snicker, just a bit caught.

Seagulls watch with mischievous eyes,
As the tide plays tricks, what a surprise!
A sand pail ponders its painted dreams,
Wishing it knew the ocean's schemes.

A lone beach chair waits, feeling fake,
Longing for sunbathers, give it a break.
Amidst the messy dance of the sea,
Is this the fun or is it just me?

Reflections in the Saltwater

In the mirror of the sea, quite strange,
A crab holds court, it wants to change.
With every wave, he takes a bow,
He's the king, 'til he meets a cow!

Fish in bowties dance with glee,
Turtles race – oh, such a spree!
Seagulls yawn as they swoop low,
"Not my lunch!" they squawk, then go.

Starfish play cards on sandy shores,
With jellyfish dealers, oh the roars!
A clam's big grin makes everyone laugh,
When he reveals his hidden gaff.

The sun dips down with a cheeky grin,
As barnacles join the ocean's din.
"Next round's on me!" the tide calls back,
While seaweed waves from its seaweed shack.

Enchantment of the Sea Glass

In a bottle of green, an octopus sighs,
With dreams of swimming under the skies.
He's found sea glass, shiny and clear,
"Hey, is that a treasure?" he shouts with cheer!

Blue and brown pieces dance and swirl,
Shells giggle as they give a twirl.
A clam ambassadors debate for fun,
"One's a gem, but the real fun's begun!"

Each color tells a story, oh so wild,
Plucked from the sea, it's a dreamy child.
Mermaids try to make necklaces bright,
"Oops! That was a fish!" they squeal in flight.

The shoreline glows with laughter and light,
As sea glass winks in the soft moonlight.
The ocean chuckles, a tune it hums,
"Let's celebrate, here the fun never slums!"

Dreamscapes in the Driftwood

Driftwood dreams drift on by,
As seagulls plan their next sly fly.
A log tells tales of far-off lands,
And daydreaming fish draw lazy strands.

"Let's have a party!" the starfish cheer,
"A driftwood raft for all, come here!"
They stack seaweed, crown, and wear,
It's a fun gala, with fish in the air.

Crabs serve snacks on plates of shells,
With guest lists bouncing like playful bells.
Anemone hosts juggle with glee,
While chatty oysters sip on sea tea.

As the tide rises, laughter fills the scene,
While dolphins perform, a sparkly routine.
The moon grins down, a jellyfish glow,
"Who knew driftwood could steal the show?"

Echoing Among the Anemones

In a pub of anemones, songs arise,
"Let's toast to the waves!" everyone cries.
A clownfish juggles his neon spheres,
While blowfish blow bubbles, soothing fears.

An octopus croons with eight-armed flair,
"Who needs a band? I've got plenty to share!"
Laughter bubbles, as the sea floor shakes,
With pufferfish playing jump rope with flakes.

A crab DJ spins seashell beats,
As sea stars blink in whimsical feats.
A turtle hops in with a beatnik strut,
"Join the wave! Don't get in a rut!"

Echoes of joy bounce off the coral,
With shrimp on the dance floor, spinning floral.
In anemone's arms, the night unfolds,
As tides of laughter burst, untold!

Serenity in the Shell's Embrace

A crab wearing glasses, so silly and bright,
Said, "I'm off to the dance, it's my glamorous night!"
But tripped on a seaweed, fell right on his back,
With fish laughing softly, he turned a bright black.

A clam shared her pearls, thought it quite a show,
While a seahorse waltzed, with an elegant glow.
"Who needs a tuxedo? Just look at my hair!"
The starfish just chuckled, "You're fishy and rare!"

An otter rolled by, eating seaweed and fries,
"Join me for lunch, I've got treats of all size!"
But the jellyfish shimmied, waved arms with delight,
"Let's have a jamboree until deep in the night!"

So here in the surf, with laughter combined,
The strangest of creatures were joyful, aligned.
A curious place, where the weirdos all sing,
In shells we find comfort, and joy's what we bring.

The Hidden Life Beneath

Beneath the blue waves, where no one can see,
Lives a lobster named Larry, a chef full of glee.
He tucked in a sea sponge, called it fine bread,
And served up his catch, with a bright wink and thread.

A sea cucumber muttered, "That looks quite a dish,
But I'm not up for algae, it's just not my wish."
"Then I'll whip up a salad, with pearls as the dress!"
The fish all agreed, "Now that's simply the best!"

From the shadows emerged, a clam with a plan,
"I'm hosting a party, now come take a stand!
Bring your crusty shell, we'll dance on the sand,
Of course if you're shy, don't get out of hand!"

So down in the depths, with giggles and cheer,
The wildest of critters just gathered right here.
With tentacles waving and laughter afloat,
This culinary scene made them all want to gloat.

Rhythms of the Rushing Waves

In the rush of the tide, where the sea foam does play,
A fish named Fred danced, in a peculiar way.
He slipped and he slid, on a wet shiny rock,
While the octopus giggled, "You're late for the clock!"

With surfboards made of shells, the gang took their ride,
While dolphins performed tricks, in the bright blue tide.
A crab flipped a coin, said, "Five bucks on blue!"
And they laughed till they cried, under skies so true.

A buoy bounced nearby, with a funny old song,
That had both fish and fowl joining right in along.
"We'll surf till the stars, let the currents decide,
At the end of the day, let's just share the tide!"

So they danced through the bubbles, and laughed by the shore,
With every big wave, they just wanted more.
Together they swam, in a symphony grand,
Where rhythm and frolic, made life oh so planned.

Gazing into the Molten Tide

As the sun started setting, the shells turned to gold,
A jellyfish pondered, "How many stories I hold?"
With a flick of her tentacles, she spun 'round in pose,
"Let's chart out the secrets that nobody knows!"

A hermit crab grumbled, "I want my own shell,
This one's much too cramped, and it smells really swell!"

While a clownfish chimed in, "You can share with me!
We'll make it a party, just wait and you'll see!"

The seagulls were squawking, "Your tides are so loud!
We prefer our own clam chowder on a cloud!"
But the sea turtles hummed, "Just chill, take a dip,
In the rays of the sunset, let's all take a trip!"

So they settled together, watched colors collide,
Finding laughter in shadows where mishaps abide.
In this molten embrace, all creatures unite,
Awash with delight in the glow of the night.

Depths of a Mutable Sanctuary

Beneath the waves, a clam once said,
"I'm tired of sand, I want a bed!"
Starfish giggled, rolling on the floor,
"You need a pillow, just not from the shore!"

Anemones waved with jellybean glee,
"What's this clam's deal, is it just me?"
Crabs cracked jokes while doing a dance,
"Being a mollusk is quite a chance!"

The octopus turned, a wise old sage,
"Be careful what you wish for, my page!"
As they laughed, a wave splashed around,
In this floating circus, joy's always found.

So if you seek humor under the sea,
Join the antics of critters wild and free!
With every tide, new tales shall dwell,
In this silly sanctuary, all is well.

Tides of Memory and Melancholy

A sea cucumber felt quite forlorn,
"I lost my sense of humor this morn!"
Starfish replied, with a grin so bright,
"Bring out your tickles, turn woe into light!"

Crab forgot where it buried its shell,
Said with a chuckle, "Oh, can't you tell?"
Fish spun around, all colors and charm,
"I can't keep track of my own alarm!"

The seaweed danced to remind us to play,
"Catch a wave, laugh it off, come what may!"
Though memories drift on a current so blue,
In the ocean's embrace, there's always a view.

So when days feel low, dive in for a swim,
With friends by your side, the light never dims!
Every wave brings back laughter and fun,
In this briny kingdom, we're never outdone.

Unraveling Waves of Wonder

In the foam, a crab crafted a joke,
"Why did the fish prefer to poke?"
Squid turned, with eyes full of surprise,
"To get to the bottom of fishy lies!"

Bubbles giggled, rising with glee,
"Tell us more, oh wise crab, you see?"
With a wave, the kelp joined the scene,
"Let's unravel the waves of our dream!"

A dolphin leaped with a splash and a song,
"Life's too short to worry; come dance along!"
Turtles joined in with their slow-motion flare,
"Let's make some memories, light as air!"

Each ripple of laughter painted the sea,
With friends around us, who could disagree?
In this world of wonder, we glide and we flow,
Forever unraveling, our joy on show.

Shell Songs and Ebbing Currents

A conch began to sing a silly tune,
"The crabs are plotting an ice cream heist soon!"
Gulls above cawed, flapping with cheer,
"Count me in! I want a scoop right here!"

Clams joined in with their softest hum,
But as they sang, something went numb!
'Ebbing currents!' one clam did chime,
"We forgot the toppings; oh, what a crime!"

Seahorses twirled with a flick of their tails,
"Pass the sprinkles and tell us some tales!"
The ocean chuckled, a giggle or two,
As they filled each shell with delights anew.

So gather your friends, both near and far,
For shell songs echo beneath the stars!
In the tides of laughter, joy finds a way,
In this watery world, let's celebrate play!

Tales from the Tidal Zone

In shells so bright, the crabs do dance,
They scuttle sideways, no time for romance.
Starfish pretend they're stuck on the floor,
"Help me up, I swear I won't ask for more!"

The sea anemones giggle with glee,
"Watch this fish, think it's running from me!"
Jellyfish dangle like jellied delight,
"Catch me if you can! Oh wait, not tonight!"

Octopuses juggle with ink in their hands,
"See my new trick? Just trying to make plans!"
A clam sings softly, but no one can tell,
"I'm the best singer, just don't ring the bell!"

So here's to the fun beneath the blue,
Where ocean's silliness shines through and through.
Join the splash party, let's laugh till we're sore,
In the tidal zone, there's always much more!

Lighthouses of the Heart

A lighthouse shines, but it's tired of duty,
Wishing for romance, not just a cutie.
"The waves are my minions, they never let up!"
It hopes for a ship with a heart-shaped cup.

A seagull swoops by with a sandwich to share,
"Watch out for the ships that don't really care!"
The wind laughs and blows, tossing hats in the air,
"Who needs a captain? Just let down your hair!"

Stars twinkle above, as they joke and they sing,
The moon winks and says, "Let the memories cling!"
Mariners chuckle as they navigate light,
"Lighthouses are dating, isn't that quite the sight?"

So guide me along, you pillars of cheer,
Of lighthouses and love, let's toast with a beer!
A beacon of joy in a world full of frights,
Together we shine, like a thousand grand lights!

Conversations with the Currents

The waves have a chat, making bubbles with cheer,
"Did you hear what the tides said? It's quite a weird year!"

They gossip about fish who dance in a jig,
"Apparently, they've begun to wear wigs!"

The seaweed chimes in, all tangled and sly,
"I once saw a dolphin that could really fly!"
They titter and cackle, the dolphins all join,
"We're headed to shore, shall we crash the sea coin?"

Crabs overheard and began to take notes,
"Did you see the seals? They're wearing new coats!"
A clam chimes in, with a shell on its back,
"I'm just here for lunch, maybe a snack!"

So next time you stroll by the edge of the sea,
Listen close to the voices, let them set you free.
Laughter and joy are just waves rolled into views,
In the currents of humor, there's always good news!

Mysteries of the Ocean Floor

Beneath the waves, the treasure chests hide,
With fish in the know, who just won't abide.
"Where's the gold?" A crab asks with winks,
"Only found by mermaids, who wear fancy blinks!"

An octopus thrills to a joke about pearls,
"They're made by oysters with very few swirls!"
The sea cucumbers roll, making quite the fuss,
"I think our next party will surely be a plus!"

Surprises abound on the ocean floor's maze,
Echoes of laughter are heard through the haze.
So come take a peek where the oddities play,
Friendship and fun in the saltwater spray!

In shadows and secrets, the mysteries call,
Embrace the delight; it's a laughter-filled ball.
With every splash and swish, let joy be the key,
For the sea is our stage, and it's filled with glee!

Conversations with the Crustaceans

In a clam shell bar, they sip on brine,
Crabs crack jokes, all in good time.
Lobsters laugh, their tails all a-twirl,
"Who wore it better?" makes their claws curl.

Shrimps tell tales of the seaweed wars,
"Front row seats, oh the villainous scores!"
One sported a hat made of kelp,
While another claimed, "I'm better than yelp!"

Mussels debate who's the best in town,
While snails just slide slowly, wearing a frown.
"Oysters are shucking, where's the great food?"
All while the tide tickles the mood.

Seashells act as microphones, quite grand,
Each crustacean with the mic in hand.
They sing songs of the ocean waves,
Creating a ruckus, oh how it saves!

The Quiet Life Beneath the Waves

Underneath where the bubbles dance,
A starfish tries to take a stance.
"Five arms are better," it made a plea,
"Why settle for none when you can have me?"

Anemones sway, giving a cheer,
"Let's have a party, bring all your gear!"
But sea cucumbers, slow as can be,
Muttered, "Partying? Please let me be!"

A blowfish puffs up with quite the flair,
"Check out my size, I'm beyond compare!"
With a wink and a smile, it takes a dive,
"Just watch my friends, the sea urchins thrive!"

The jellyfish glow, an elegant sight,
But they giggle, "I float, isn't it light?"
Life beneath waves, so comically trite,
Turns into laughter, oh what a night!

Beneath the Barnacle Skies

Beneath the sky made of barnacle grit,
Seahorses argue who's more of a hit.
One claims its tail has a swirling design,
The other just puffs, "I'm a real fine line!"

The octopus juggles with curious glee,
Throwing seaweed like it's a spree.
"Catch my best moves!" it boldly declares,
While fish shake their scales, avoiding repairs.

An elder whale with wisdom to spare,
Whispers to shells, delighting in air.
"Remember the times we used to play?
Now here comes the tide, ruining our day!"

Starry night over the barnacle films,
It's no wonder everyone just yells.
Crabs in tuxedos, acting so prim,
Under barnacle skies, the fun won't dim!

Glimmers in the Shallow Water

In the shallows where secrets gleam,
Sand dollars giggle, living the dream.
"Catch me if you can!" they call out in jest,
While silver fish dart, they're clearly the best.

A sea star spins tales of how it got lost,
"I took a wrong turn, oh, what a cost!"
Every barnacle chuckles, it's quite the show,
As a dolphin pops up, putting on a bow.

Clams play cards with shells, the stakes are high,
"Well, I'll just bluff!" says one with a sigh.
The tide rolls in, a tidal wave crash,
"Hold your hand tight, or you'll lose in a flash!"

Glimmers arise, where the fun never ends,
Life in the shallows, oh how it bends.
With laughter and cheer, the sea does impart,
Joyful moments—a whimsical art!

Songs Beneath the Solstice

The crab sings a tune, a tap-dance so bright,
While sea stars cheer with some shells in their sight.
A clam joins the band as it claps with its shell,
Creating a symphony, oh, what a swell!

A jellyfish hums with a wobbly grin,
While fish flip and flop, showing off in a spin.
Gulls laugh out loud as they swoop down for fish,
A melodious mess, it's quite the swish!

Seahorses dance in a boogie so fine,
While hermit crabs hustle and try to outshine.
Each wave is a stage for this wild, funny show,
As the sun sets down with an orange-hued glow.

In the end, all tire, they call it a night,
With a wink from the tide as it dims the last light.
So here's to the songs, so funny and bright,
In a world full of giggles, under stars shining white.

Murmurs at the Edge of the Shore

The sand piper pranced with a bouncy little hop,
While the seaweed swayed with its own little pop.
A conch shell proclaimed, 'Join the grand parade!'
And the crabs all scuttled, 'Let's dance, don't be afraid!'

The tide comes in, with a foamy sequence,
Tickling toes, the tide brings a fresh, salty sense.
Seagulls announce, 'What's this splashing delight?'
As fish make a splash, in a jump gone awry.

A barnacle shouted, 'Hey, what's that you wear?'
As the flounder struggled to groom its own hair.
A clam piped up with a grin quite absurd,
'Last time I checked, you were just a big turd!'

The beach was a laugh, a giggle-filled spree,
As shells and the tide sparked joy in the sea.
Each wave brought a chuckle, a splashy surprise,
With laughter and sunlight beneath brilliant skies.

The Lullaby of Coral Reefs

In the coral garden, a fish took a nap,
While a turtle hummed, like a grandpa on a flap.
Starfish giggled, trading tickles in style,
While the anemone winked with a bubbly smile.

An octopus crafted a hat made of kelp,
And the seahorses cheered, 'Oh, that's quite a yelp!'
A porcupine fish puffed, trying to show,
That playing it cool is just part of the flow.

Clownfish chuckled at their own silly mask,
'Why be too serious? Just grab us a flask!'
A conch started rapping, with beats oh so thrifty,
As the shrimp all replied, 'This groove is quite nifty!'

As night falls on the reef, under starlit beams,
The fish still keep dancing, lost deep in their dreams.
With a lullaby sung by the waves and the foam,
In a world of mirth, they've found their sweet home.

Beneath the Crystalline Surface

Bubbles rise up with a pop and a fizz,
As the sea cucumbers wiggle with ease.
Shrimps take a stroll, wearing hats made of shell,
While the clownfish giggle, in their own little spell.

The dolphins arrive with a splash and a cheer,
Doing flips and spins, spreading giggles near.
An urchin chimed in, 'This party's so bright!'
With colors ablaze, it's a laugh every night.

The flatfish were trying to blend in the sand,
While the puffers were chasing a rogue rubber band.
A turbot declared, 'Let's dance to the tide!'
With every wave crashing, they laughed at their pride.

Under moonlight, the reef basks in the glow,
Each creature a star in the ultimate show.
With bubbles and laughter, we swim and we play,
In this watery world, we're just here for the sway.

Songs of the Sheltered Shore

The crab wore a hat, oh what a sight,
Danced on the sand, his moves were bright.
A seagull squawked, 'You're stealing my show!'
But the crab just laughed, said, 'Let's go, bro!'

The seaweed waved, with a jellyfish friend,
They played hide and seek, just around the bend.
"Oh no, you're 'stinging' me!" the seaweed did tease,
But the jelly's just giggling, enjoying the breeze.

A starfish debated with a clam on the floor,
"Who's got more arms?" was the question they bore.
The clam just replied, "I'm doing just fine,
With my one sturdy shell, and a pearly design!"

So let's raise a shell to our shelled pals so free,
In their sandy kingdom beneath the sea.
Where laughter abounds, even crabs can play,
On this sheltered shore, where we all can stay.

Echoes Beneath the Surface

A fish tried to sing, but got caught in a net,
Its voice was a bubble, not a tune to forget.
"Oh gill me a break!" was the fish's keen cry,
While the octopus giggled, from up high nearby.

A scallop dressed up for a fancy sea ball,
With pearls 'round its neck, it was ready to sprawl.
But tripped on a sea cucumber, what a surprise,
The dance floor erupted with delightful cries.

The sea urchin laughed, hiding spikes in its shell,
"Life's just a poke, so let's party and swell!"
The hermit crab chimed in, "I'll bring the snacks,
Just don't eat my home, or I'll have to relax!"

So dive into fun, where the bubbles do twirl,
In a world full of giggles, let the sea unfurl.
With friends by your side, what a magical ride,
As the echoes of laughter drift far and wide.

Secrets of the Rock Pool

A sea star confessed, with a wink and a grin,
"I lost all my spots, where do I begin?"
The anemone giggled, swaying to and fro,
"Just grab a paintbrush, and put on a show!"

The hermit crab grumbled, "This home's not my style,
I need something flashy to go the extra mile."
A barnacle scoffed, "You think that you're slick?
Your shell's barely stylish, it's really quite sick!"

A shrimp told a tale of treasure and gold,
But he hid in a bubble, so timid and cold.
"Come join in the fun, don't just stand there and puff,
Or I'll have to remind you, that I'm super tough!"

In these rock pool antics, where the funny things bloom,
Life's secrets unfold with a shimmer and zoom.
Amidst all the laughter, with friends hand in fin,
Every tidepool moment, is where we begin.

Murmurs from the Ocean's Edge

A dolphin delighted, with flips that amaze,
While a seagull squawked, in awe of the display.
"Let's start a band!" the flippered one said,
And the gull just squawked, "I'll play with my head!"

The tide rolled in, bringing jokes on a wave,
Where sea creatures gathered, feeling so brave.
"We'll tell tales so tall, you won't believe your eyes,
Like the octopus in boots who won first prize!"

The fish rolled their eyes, shared a wink with a blink,
"We follow the tide, it's a fun little link.
So let's make waves with laughter and cheer,
At the ocean's edge, there's nothing to fear!"

From shells to the sand, in the bright sun's glow,
The giggles abound, as the ocean flows.
So come join the fun, with your friends by your side,
At the edge of the ocean, where joy is our guide.

The Dance of the Dunes

On sandy hills, the crabs do prance,
With sideways shuffles, oh what a dance!
They wiggle and jiggle, in comical glee,
Who knew the beach held such jubilee?

The seagulls squawk with a laughter so loud,
As the tides roll in, they gather in crowds.
With beaks like comedians, they steal our fries,
Their antics bring tears, oh how we all sigh!

A starfish wearing a sunhat so bright,
Waves hello with a wave, oh what a sight!
The beach ball bounces, but where will it land?
It keeps rolling away, aren't tides just grand?

With footprints in sand, we stroll hand in hand,
The goofy sea creatures, we just can't withstand.
As the sun sets low, the laughter won't cease,
In this grand ballroom of nature, we find our peace.

Silent Voices of the Coastal Heart

How turtles meander, slow and serene,
While little fish dart, in swims a routine.
They gossip and giggle, beneath seaweed tides,
A secretive world where humor abides.

The conch shells chant, in whispers and sighs,
Sharing tales of sailors and their wild lies.
The gulls interrupt with a squawk—what a show!
They claim all the drama, but we really know!

A clam tried to dance, but it couldn't find feet,
It just sat there laughing, what a funny feat!
The sea foam giggles as bubbles depart,
In this cackling ocean, who plays the true part?

So gather your friends, let the laughter commence,
For the shoreline sets stage for a comical dance.
With each crashing wave, we join in the fun,
In this heart of the coast, we're never outrun.

Echoes of the Sea's Embrace

The ocean calls out with a giggle and splash,
As shells tell their secrets in bubbles of trash.
A dolphin does flips, in joy it delights,
Telling fish jokes on those moonlit nights.

A sea cucumber lounges, oh what a sight!
Not a care in the world, it sleeps through the night.
The octopus chuckles, its arms in a knot,
Creating silly shapes, giving us quite a plot.

Anemones wave with a breeze in delight,
While a crab in a bowtie struts left and right.
The seabirds all cackle, as if in a play,
With their feathery antics, they brighten the day.

So join in the fun, embrace all the cheer,
In this watery world, there's nothing to fear.
With laughter and joy, let's dance with the tides,
In echoes of laughter, our spirit abides.

Secrets of the Shallow Waters

In the shallows, where giggles frolic and roam,
Bubbles emerge like thoughts of home.
A hermit crab sneezes, oh what a surprise,
With shell-flipping laughter, it wipes its small eyes.

Corals play hide-and-seek with the sun,
While clams throw a party, oh it's so much fun!
The minnows all join in on the scene,
Creating a splash with a twist—what a dream!

The jellyfish jiggle, like jello gone wild,
Drifting through currents, oh what a child!
From starfish with jokes to shrimp with their tales,
This lively brigade of sea life never fails.

So dive in the waters, where laughter takes flight,
In these shallow realms, joy shines so bright.
With secrets and stories, the tides start to play,
In this ocean of fun, we'll surf the day away.

Shifting Patterns of Coastal Dreams

Sandcastles crumbled, oh what a mess,
A crab in my pocket, that's quite the dress!
Seagulls are teasing, they dive and they fly,
I dropped my sandwich, oh me, oh my!

The tide rolls in, pulls my socks away,
Splashing my toes, it's a funny ballet.
The starfish are laughing, they're quite the jest,
With all of this chaos, I'm feeling quite blessed.

A clam's got my phone, and it won't let go,
As waves break around me, I start to bestow.
A giggle ensues, from a fish in disguise,
"Don't look at me funny with those googly eyes!"

As I toss back a shell, it flies like a plane,
Lands on a seagull who squawks in disdain.
"Oh, what a day!" I declare with a cheer,
In the dream of the coast, all my worries disappear.

Whims of the Merrymaking Sea

The ocean is dancing, what a quirky show,
Seaweed doing limbo, look at it go!
Crabs in tuxedos, all prim and so neat,
Tap dancing on rocks, what a lavish feat!

The jellyfish waltz, with no clue at all,
Bumping and gliding, down they fall.
"I swear I can swim," one sea otter croons,
As a wave takes him under, to sing with the tunes.

Bubbles are popping like fireworks bright,
Every splash brings laughter, what a lovely sight!
Beach balls are flying, tied up with glee,
While dolphins are teaching a cha-cha, whee!

Guess what! The tide's doing the moonwalk tonight,
A splash from the seal makes it all feel just right.
Frolicsome fishes join in the hilarity,
In the carnival sea, pure absurdity!

Beneath a Canopy of Kelp

Kelp fronds are swinging, a wacky spree,
Seahorses tango, as happy as can be!
A clam plays the drums on an old, sunken ship,
While octopuses juggle with a flip and a skip.

The tide pulls and tugs like a playful friend,
A squirrel in a shell thinks this is the end.
"Help!" he exclaims, "I'm having a ball!"
As jellybeans float by, in this underwater hall.

Crabs with sunglasses pose for the shot,
"Say cheese!" they all clack, what a silly plot!
The urchins are stifling giggles and snorts,
While schools of fish throw all amusing reports.

Down in the deep where the laughter can swell,
The dance of the reef casts a goofy spell.
With smiles and glee, it's a comical ride,
In a world full of playfulness, I happily glide.

Rhapsody of the Rolling Surf

The surf is a symphony, loud and absurd,
Where clams sing their woes, it's quite the weird word.
Fish throw a concert, scales shining bright,
As bubbles join in, floating up with delight.

The sea foam erupts with giggles and glee,
"A jellyfish stole my towel!" cries she.
A dolphin, all fancy, flips high in the air,
While starfish applaud without a single care.

Rolling waves tumble, but do they complain?
"More sand in my sandwich!" they chant with disdain.
Seagulls join in, as they flap and they flap,
"Bring us the snacks!" they squawk in a flap.

As tides hum a tune, with rhythms to sway,
I dance with the currents, come join in the play!
The coast is a chorus, where laughter holds sway,
In the rhapsody rolling, it's all fun today!

Songlines of the Changing Tide

In the tidepool, crabs dance quick,
With tiny feet that make us tick.
Starfish giggle, sticking tight,
As seaweed pranks in morning light.

Fish make faces, all a sight,
As snails spin tales of silly fright.
The mollusks laugh, they can't look cool,
With shells so shiny, who's the fool?

Anemone sways like it's on the run,
While shrimp tell jokes, just for fun.
Gulls overhead swoop down, what's the fuss?
"Did you see the crab? He made a fuss!"

The hermit crabs wear different shells,
Each one thinks they're ringing bells.
Nature smiles in colors bright,
In the tidepool, all feels right!

Nurtured by the Ocean's Breath

Oh, the clams, they play peek-a-boo,
While sea urchins just sip their brew.
Octopus tickles with ink so sly,
"Can you beat that?" they all reply.

Barnacles grumble, stuck on rocks,
While wrasses tease with funny socks.
Seagulls squawk, thinking they rule,
But it's the jellyfish that play it cool.

A crab in a hurry, thinks it's a race,
With a shrimp on its tail, both quick in pace.
They slide on stones, laughing with glee,
"What's the rush?" says a wise old sea bee.

With each wave that splashes ashore,
The creatures giggle, demanding more.
In the ocean's pulse, there's joy to be,
Where each salty splash brings chuckles, you see!

Driftwood Diaries

On a driftwood log, there lies a tale,
Of crabs playing tag in the salty gale.
Seagulls perched, with sass and flair,
    Swooping low without a care.

The seaweed dances, waving its green,
Tickling fishes wherever they've been.
Starfish chat about their last meal,
    "What tasted better? You've got to feel!"

Oh, and the dolphins, jumping high,
Saying, "What's next? Another pie in the sky!"
With giggles and splashes throughout the day,
    Life in the tide, a comical play.

Every wave carries a story or joke,
As coastal critters gather and poke.
Each driftwood piece, a seat for the fun,
In our ocean's diary, every verse runs!

The Ballet of Crashing Waves

Waves perform a splashing dance,
Crabs tap their feet, given the chance.
The seafoam spins with a frothy grace,
While clams cheer on, making their case.

Fish flip and flounder, in a chaotic spin,
"I'll dance too, don't let me in!"
The sea cucumber wobbles along,
With a mollusk's croon like a silly song.

A plankton jester prances near,
Fish laugh so hard, shed a tear.
Flip-flopping laughter, coast to coast,
What sea creature is trying to boast?

Seashells clink in a mariner's tune,
While sea stars twinkle under the moon.
With a splash and a crash, the ballet rolls on,
In the tide's warm embrace, the fun goes on!

Colors of the Tidal Region

In the seaweed's dance, a cheeky crab thrived,
Wearing a kelp crown, he felt quite alive.
With polka-dot fish and a bright yellow ray,
They threw a wild party, splashing away.

Octopus served snacks on a shell made of pearl,
While sea cucumbers twirled in a whirl.
The starfish clapped with its five little arms,
Juggling sea urchins, oh what funny charms!

A clam told a joke, but it turned out to be,
A little too salty for all to agree.
They laughed until bubbles rose to the top,
In this vibrant region, no one could stop!

So when the tide ebbs and the sun's shining bright,
Remember the laughter beneath waves of delight.
Colors abound where the ocean is free,
In this jolly place, who wouldn't want to be?

Fragments of Nautical Folklore

A turtle once claimed it could sing like a whale,
But only produced a rather loud wail.
The gulls rolled their eyes, said, 'Not quite right!'
And formed a band that played through the night.

"Once a fish danced on the back of a seal,
And they spun 'round, what a surreal reel!"
The octopus laughed, served squid balls on a tray,
While the shells joined in, hip-hip-hooray!

Mermaids giggled, hiding their hair in the foam,
They whispered of sailors, always far from home.
Each tale a delight, like candy from the sea,
With more twists and turns than a seaweed spree!

So gather 'round if you're in for a laugh,
From krakens to pixies, we'll split our sides in half.
Nautical tales keep the ocean alive,
With humor unending, where all creatures thrive!

Serenades of the Scale

In a chorus of fish, they sang 'Let's unite!'
With scales that could shimmer, a dazzling sight.
But the little guppy forgot all the words,
And just bubbled up, in a flurry of blurs.

The bass led the tune, trying hard not to flounder,
While the octopus played a tune on aounder.
The flute fish floated, all graceful and grand,
Until a shrimp sneezed and messed up the band!

They practiced all day, but the notes went awry,
As the seabed echoed their laughter and sighs.
"Just follow the beat of the waves," cried the kite,
And soon every creature felt merry and light.

So join in the fun, let your laughter resound,
In the serenades where friendships abound.
Underwater concerts, a spectacle bright,
With giggles and gurgles, oh what sheer delight!

Secrets in the Swell

Beneath the surf, a secretive eel,
Wore a hat made of seaweed, oh what a deal!
He fancied himself quite the stylish sort,
Until a wave hit him, and he fell out of port.

A playful dolphin jumped high in the sky,
Said, "Join me for fun, we'll dance and we'll fly!"
But under the surface, a crab played it cool,
Offering potions brewed in a shell, what a tool!

The sea turtle chuckled, "Oh, not that again!"
"Last time you pulled in an octopus friend!"
So they all agreed to keep secrets tight,
In the swell of the ocean, under moonlight.

With bubbles for laughter and foam for their tears,
They shared tiny tales that no one else hears.
For laughter is timeless, in currents and flows,
In the heart of the waves, true magic still grows!

Illuminations of an Aquatic Realm

Beneath the waves, a crab in a hat,
Dances and twirls, imagine that!
A fish in a tux gives a cheeky grin,
While a seaweed wig is a win-win-win!

A clam throws a party, all shells on parade,
With jellyfish jellies that never do fade.
"And who brought the snacks?" a starfish inquires,
"Sweet plankton bites, and some sea-salt fires!"

The octopus juggles with eight quirky hands,
As seagulls dive in for unsanctioned bands.
The rhythm is crazy, the joy is so clear,
A splash here, a laugh there, it's the best time of year!

When the tide pulls back, and the party gets low,
They all reminisce about the waves and the glow.
A crab sighs, "I wish we could dance until dawn!"
But the sun's peeking in, and so the fun's gone!

Treasures in the Coastal Shadows

In a nook by the rocks, a treasure chest waits,
Full of lost socks and some curious weights.
"Why would anyone keep these?" the gulls start to laugh,
"Did they lose their sense, or just take a wrong path?"

Starfish gossip about a sock on a fish,
That made quite the rumor — oh, what a big swish!
A crab with a monocle joins in the quest,
"To find out the truth, let's put them to rest!"

They venture through shadows, with giggles and glee,
Past the sneaky sea cucumber, oh what a spree!
Finding old treasures, they cheer and they shout,
"Who knew beachcombing would be so much fun out?"

Then back to the beach, with the suns starting to set,
They share stories of find, making memories yet.
With laughter and banter, they cradle the tide,
For treasures in shadows are best when they're spied!

The Language of Rockpools

In the rockpools, critters exchange little jokes,
"Why did the sea urchin cross the sea floor?" it pokes.
"To get to the other tide!" they all burst with glee,
While a clam rolls its eyes, "Can't sea urchins see?"

Anemones giggle as they sway side to side,
"Tangled up in laughter, we won't let tides hide!"
A shrimp with a top hat declares it's quite clear,
"The best kind of chatter, is salty with cheer!"

They make up a language of bubbles and waves,
Translate all meanings in colorful braves.
A sea star offers, "Join in the fun,
And let's draft a poem like the ones we've spun!"

With shells for the verses, and seafoam for rhyme,
Each tidepool grows louder, getting better with time.
As the sun starts to sink, they know one thing right,
Their friendship is language, pure joy in the light!

Patterns in the Surf

As the surf rolls in, with a whimsical grin,
They play hopscotch on waves, let the laughter begin.
A jellyfish shimmies, gliding in style,
Making patterns with friends that stretch every mile!

A dolphin spots shells, bright blue and so round,
Counts them with joy, leaps high from the ground.
With splashes of color, they cheer and they chant,
"Who knew the ocean could throw such a dance?"

Sand dollar dancers twist in the foam,
Creating a spectacle, an aquatic home.
As crabs join the line, clickety-clack,
They all twirl together, no holding them back!

But the tide begins tugging, party's nearly through,
With every wave crashing, they giggle and coo.
"We'll catch the next tide, when the fun's out to play,
The patterns we made will just wash away!"

www.ingramcontent.com/pod-product-compliance
Lightning Source LLC
Chambersburg PA
CBHW060145230426
43661CB00003B/578